Ripley's Believe It or Not!

Developed and produced by Ripley Publishing Ltd

This edition published and distributed by:

Mason Crest
450 Parkway Drive, Suite D, Broomall, PA 19008
www.masoncrest.com

Printed and bound in the United States of America

First printing
9 8 7 6 5 4 3 2 1

Ripley's Believe It or Not!
Unbelievable Feats
ISBN: 978-1-4222-2784-8 (hardback)
ISBN: 978-1-4222-9045-3 (e-book)
Ripley's Believe It or Not!—Complete 8 Title Series
ISBN: 978-1-4222-2979-8

Cataloging-in-Publication Data on file with the Library of Congress

PUBLISHER'S NOTE
While every effort has been made to verify the accuracy of the entries in this book, the
Publishers cannot be held responsible for any errors contained in the work. They would
be glad to receive any information from readers.

WARNING
Some of the stunts and activities in this book are undertaken by experts and should not
be attempted by anyone without adequate training and supervision.

Ripley's Believe It or Not!

Strikingly True

UNBELIEVABLE FEATS

www.MasonCrest.com

UNBELIEVABLE FEATS

Prepare to be amazed by the most spectacular

achievements! Find out about extraordinary

exploits. Discover the guy who surfed for

26 hours straight, the man who walked across

a 1,000-ft (305-m) highline, and remarkable

tales of the Olympic Games.

Dean Potter walked across a highline
100 ft (30 m) long over 1,000 ft (305 m)
from the ground...

Ripley's — **Believe It or Not!®** Unbelievable feats

GREAT ESCAPES

At 32 years old, Akash Awasthi is already one of the most daring escapologists in India, risking life and limb to escape from a burning haystack, a locked box deep underwater, and a coffin placed in the path of a speeding truck.

He has also ridden a motorbike through the packed city streets of Trivandrum, Kerala, while blindfolded. He is following in the footsteps of his father, Anand Awasthi, one of the most famous magicians in the country.

1

THE GREAT FIRE ESCAPE

Akash's most dangerous feat is to escape from a giant burning haystack. First he is bound with 25 locks and a 25-ft-long (7.5-m) chain, and hoisted into the air on a 120-ft (37-m) crane.

Akash is hoisted into the air by a 120-ft (37-m) crane.

2

Akash fights his way out of the burning haystack, which becomes an inferno within seconds.

UNDERWATER ESCAPE

Akash has twice taken on the famous underwater box escape. It was first performed by the legendary Harry Houdini in 1912 in New York, and he took 57 seconds to free himself. Akash's father also performed the stunt in 1970, taking 40 seconds to emerge. This escape is one of the most dangerous performed by escapologists. In 1983, Dean Gunnarson failed to escape from a coffin submerged in a Canadian river and stopped breathing before being resuscitated. In his first attempt at the underwater record in Hyderabad, Akash took just 15 seconds to reach the surface. His second attempt was in the harbor at Trivandrum. Handcuffed and chained, he was locked inside a box and lowered into water 150 ft (46 m) deep. Akash surfaced after only a few seconds. When the box was retrieved from the water, it was intact, with the chains and handcuffs still inside.

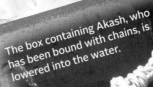

The box containing Akash, who has been bound with chains, is lowered into the water.

The fearless escapologist emerges from the locked box.

Akash emerges from the flames, unchained, moments before the haystack is completely engulfed. He is tended to by volunteers.

③

FAMOUS ESCAPES

1. Matt the Knife (U.S.A.) took just 11 seconds to free himself from handcuffs while underwater.

2. Dorothy Dietrich (U.S.A.) escaped from a straitjacket while suspended from a burning rope hundreds of feet in the air.

3. Dean Gunnarson (Canada) escaped from a straitjacket while hanging upside down from a trapeze 726 ft (221 m) above the gorge of the Hoover Dam.

4. David Merlini (Hungary) escaped from a shark-filled pool while in a straitjacket, weights, and restraints.

5. Zdenek Bradac (Czech Republic) escaped from a pair of real police handcuffs in 1.6 seconds.

6. David Straitjacket (U.K.) escaped from a straitjacket while on stilts in 1 minute 38 seconds.

7. David Blaine (U.S.A.) took 15 minutes to free himself from shackles and a gyroscope that had been spinning him around 50 ft (15 m) above Times Square, New York, for 52 hours.

Ripley's—
Believe It or Not!
unbelievable feats

Mighty Mouth

A man in Lagos, Nigeria, lifts a bar carrying 110 lb (50 kg) of iron weights with his mouth!

solo sailor At age 16, Jessica Watson of Queensland, Australia, finished a 210-day, 23,000-nautical-mile (42,600-km), solo, nonstop, and unassisted voyage around the world. In her 34-ft-long (10-m) yacht *Ella's Pink Lady*, she battled 39-ft (12-m) swells and a ripped sail, and ate 576 chocolate bars.

jail jaunt In June 2009, 194 French inmates made a 1,430-mi (2,300-km) bicycle trip through the country in a prisoners' Tour de France.

head-to-head Croatian tennis player Goran Ivanisevic needed stitches when he tried to head the ball over the net at the 1998 Canadian Open, only to bang heads with his doubles partner Mark Philippoussis, who had tried to do the same thing. Philippoussis got away with only a bruised forehead.

dodgeball tournament In October 2009, more than 235 teams in three divisions competed in a dodgeball tournament in Richmond, Virginia, involving more than 4,000 players.

novice at 90 Ninety-year-old Mary Tattersall from West Yorkshire, England, hit a hole-in-one at a golf course near Bradford in 2010. She had been playing golf for only two years.

world cup miss Spain's international goalkeeper Santiago Cañizares missed the 2002 soccer World Cup after dropping a bottle of aftershave onto his right foot, severing one of his tendons.

board marathon A team of ten wakeboarders (a cross between waterskiing and surfing) completed 1,448 laps of a Cincinnati, Ohio, cable wakeboard park in 24 hours in June 2010. They traveled just over 506 mi (814 km)—roughly the distance from Cincinnati to Atlanta, Georgia.

delayed game Twenty-one years after a 1989 New Jersey high-school hockey championship game between Delbarton and St. Joseph's was canceled because of a measles outbreak, the players—now in their late thirties—finally took to the ice to play the deciding game for charity.

surf club The Palestinian territory's Gaza Strip has its own surf club, which was founded after a Jewish surfer donated a dozen surfboards to the community.

fast match In October 2009, Jo-Wilfried Tsonga of France and Spain's Fernando Verdasco played a tennis match on board a train traveling at 268 mph (431 km/h). The mini-tennis court was laid out in one of Shanghai's high-speed Maglev trains, where the players were traveling faster than their serves.

round-the-world In 2010, 34-year-old Vin Cox from Cornwall, England, cycled 18,225 mi (29,330 km) around the world in just 163 days. Starting and finishing his journey in London, he took 12 plane and boat transfers, crossed six continents—Europe, (northern) Africa, Asia, Australia, South America, and North America—and cycled through 17 countries.

big haul In August 2010, Jeff Kolodzinski caught 2,160 fish—mostly small bluegills and perch—from Lake Minnetonka, Minnesota, in a 24-hour period.

one-legged wrestler Michigan-based Zach "Tenacious Z" Gowen, who lost his leg at age eight, made his debut at 19 as a one-legged professional wrestler.

thrown away Jesus Leonardo of Wanaque, New Jersey, earns about $45,000 a year examining discarded horse-racing tickets for winning stubs accidentally thrown away.

insect aside Spotting that an insect had landed on his ball at the 1950 U.S. Open Golf Championship, Lloyd Mangrum of the United States instinctively picked up the ball and flicked the insect away. However, he was penalized two strokes for his misdemeanor, which ultimately cost him the title.

blind catch Sheila Penfold, a legally blind grandmother from London, England, caught a catfish that weighed in at a whopping 214 lb (97 kg) and measured 8 ft 2 in (2.5 m) long on Spain's Ebro River in January 2010. It took Mrs. Penfold, who stands just 5 ft 3 in (1.6 m) tall, 30 minutes to reel in the monster.

master jockey Since 1974, Canadian jockey Russell Baze has won more than 11,000 horse races. In the space of just two days—October 17 and 18, 2007—he won no fewer than 11 races.

seven out In 2009, in his first game as a pitcher for the St. Louis Cardinals, John Smoltz struck out seven hitters in a row—something he had never managed to do in 708 trips to the mound with his previous team, the Atlanta Braves.

first female In 2010, Kelly Kulick of the United States became the first woman to qualify for the Professional Bowlers' Association's Tournament of Champions—and she went on to beat an all-male field of 62 to claim the title.

extra load In 2009, British former soldier Kez Dunkley ran the 26.2-mi (42-km) Leicester Marathon in 5 hours 53 minutes with an 84-lb (38-kg) tumble-drier strapped to his back. The previous year he had run the race with a bag of cement on his back.

BIKE CLIMB

In November 2010, Colombian cyclist Javier Zapata rode up the 649 steps of the Piedra del Peñol monolithic formation in Guatapé, Colombia, in just 43 minutes. Zapata is no stranger to epic climbs. In 2003, he rode his bike up the 1,318 stairs of Mexico City's Torre Mayor, the tallest building in Latin America.

Bill emerges from the seawater following his surfing extravaganza with bloodshot eyes and dusted in salt.

SURF'S UP!

Surfer extraordinaire Bill Laity of San Clemente, California, surfed for 26 hours straight at the state's Huntington Beach in November 2010, during which time he caught 147 waves.

Bill paddled his board into the water at 7.24 a.m. on a Saturday morning—he didn't stop surfing until 9.26 a.m. on Sunday!

The super-surfer's fingers appear severely wrinkled as a result of being submerged in the water for 26 hours straight.

Ripley's Believe It or Not® unbelievable feats

AIRBED RACE

At the annual Glen Nevis River Race in Scotland, competitors on inflatable airbeds don helmets and lifejackets to navigate a treacherous 1½-mi (2.4-km) course along the Glen Nevis River, tackling white-water torrents, rapids, and even a 30-ft (9-m) waterfall.

R bowling star Retired high-school principal Allen Meyer of Toronto, Canada, was still bowling twice a week in a league that he ran at the age of 106.

R foul ball After years of attending Philadelphia Phillies baseball games, Steve Monforto made a great grab to catch his first foul ball. He high-fived his three-year-old daughter Emily and handed her the prize ball... which she then threw back over the railing! The family still went home with a ball after Phillies officials saw what happened and took a ball up to him. What's more, spectators threw back every foul ball caught for the remainder of the game so that Emily didn't feel bad for losing her dad the special ball.

R extreme hole The "Extreme 19th" hole at the Legend Golf and Safari Resort in Limpopo, South Africa, has a tee-off on a mountain that is accessible only by helicopter—and sits 1,300 ft (400 m) above a green designed in the shape of the continent of Africa. In 2008, Ireland's Padraig Harrington became the first golfer to make a par-3 at this hole.

R welly wanging Under the British rules of "welly wanging" (or gum-boot throwing), competitors take a maximum run-up of 42 paces before hurling a size 9, non-steel toecap gum boot through the air as far as possible. Finland's Jouni Viljanen has hurled a gum boot more than 208 ft (64 m).

R anvil blast In the U.S. sport of competitive anvil shooting, participants use black gunpowder to launch 100-lb (45-kg) anvils up to 200 ft (60 m) into the air. One anvil is placed upside down on the ground, the brick-shaped cavity in its underside is filled with gunpowder, and then a second anvil is placed on top of it. A fuse is lit—and the anvil-shooter runs as fast as he can out of the blast radius.

R rabbit jumping As well as pioneering show jumping, where horses clear obstacles, Sweden established the sport of rabbit jumping, in which domestic rabbits are trained to jump miniature fences without touching them.

R double faults In her first-round ladies' singles match at Wimbledon in 1957, Brazilian tennis player Miss M. de Amorim began by serving 17 consecutive double faults.

R flying kayak Miles Daisher of Twin Falls, Idaho, paddles a kayak—across the sky at an altitude of 13,000 ft (4,000 m). The daredevil has invented a new sport, skyaking, a combination of skydiving and kayaking. Sitting in his kayak he jumps from a plane, pulls the chute at about 5,000 ft (1,525 m), and descends at nearly 100 mph (160 km/h), reducing to half that speed as he finally swoops to land spectacularly on water.

R solo row In her 19-ft-long (5.8-m) rowboat *Liv*, Katie Spotz, 22, from Mentor, Ohio, rowed solo 2,817 mi (4,533 km) across the Atlantic Ocean from Dakar, Senegal, to Georgetown, Guyana, in just over 70 days in 2010. Previously she has swum the entire 325-mi (520-km) length of the Allegheny River, run 150 mi (240 km) across the Mojave and Colorado deserts, and cycled 3,300 mi (5,310 km) across the United States from Seattle, Washington, to Washington, D.C.

FIERY BULL

In a festival dating back to the 16th century, a Bull of Fire runs through the streets of Medinaceli, Spain. The bull's body is covered in mud to protect it from burns and it wears an iron frame on its horns that bears two torches. The bull is chased through the streets until the torches go out.

Cold Climb

In February 2010, Andreas Spak from Norway, Christian Pondella from California, and Canadian Will Gadd became the first adventurers to scale the Vøringfossen waterfall in Norway, one of the highest in Europe. In warmer weather, the water surges at 40 ft (12 m) per second, but winter temperatures of 5°F (−15°C) transformed the torrent into a 650-ft (198-m) ice skyscraper.

unbelievable feats

Ripley's
Believe It or Not!

The modern Olympic Games were established by a Frenchman—Baron de Coubertin—who was inspired by the ancient Greek competition of the same name.

They are hosted by different countries and, with the exception of three cancellations due to world wars (in 1916, 1940, and 1944), have been staged every four years since 1896. Both Summer and Winter Games are held, and today more than 13,000 athletes compete in 400 events representing 35 sports. While every Olympics delivers great tales of sporting prowess, it is perhaps some of the lesser-known tales that are the most remarkable...

THE ANCIENT OLYMPICS

Contested between representatives of several city states and kingdoms, the Ancient Olympics were staged every four years from 776BC until AD393, when Roman Emperor Theodosius banned them on the grounds that they were a pagan ritual. Believe it or not...

• The Emperor Nero of Rome competed in the AD66 Olympics, accompanied by 5,000 bodyguards, and won every event in which he took part.

• All the competitors at the Ancient Olympics were men, and they competed naked.

• Among the more unusual events was a contest for trumpeters.

• Three-time Olympic champions had statues erected in their honor and were offered exemption from taxation.

• Centurions demonstrated their speed and strength in races run in full suits of armor.

• The Pankration, or all-in wrestling, allowed any moves, including strangling your opponent.

• The 2004 Olympic marathon in Athens was raced over the same historic course first run by the messenger Pheidippides in 490BC when he announced the Greek victory over Persia in the Battle of Marathon.

THE EARLY DAYS

big chill The swimming races at the 1896 Athens Olympics were held in the Mediterranean Sea, which was so cold that many competitors, numb from the chill, gave up and had to be rescued by boat.

mystery cox To reduce the weight in their boat, Dutch pair Francois Antoine Brandt and Roelof Klein recruited a young French boy—believed to be about seven years old—to act as their coxswain in the rowing final at the 1900 Paris Olympics. The mystery boy helped them to win the Olympic title but then vanished into thin air and his name was never recorded.

the pits! The track and field events at the 1900 Paris Olympics were staged on rough ground in the Bois de Boulogne—a large park on the edge of the city—where facilities were so basic that the jumpers had to dig their own pits and the obstacles for the men's 400 meters hurdles were 30-ft-long (9-m) utility poles.

short distance Women were not allowed to compete in track and field events at the Olympics until 1928. However, some collapsed at the end of the 800 meters in that year so they were subsequently banned from running in races beyond 200 meters until 1960.

how far? During the first several modern Olympics, the marathon was an approximate distance. In 1908, the British royal family requested that the marathon start at Windsor Castle so that the royal children could see its start. The distance from Windsor Castle to the Olympic Stadium was 26 miles and 385 yd. In 1924, this distance became the standard length of a marathon.

art prizes No medals were awarded at the 1900 Paris Olympics—winners were given pieces of art instead. At this, the second of the modern Olympics, more athletes than spectators attended the Games.

OLYMPIC ODDITIES

not allowed Harvard University refused to give student James B. Connolly eight weeks' leave of absence in order to compete in the 1896 Olympics in Greece. So he resigned from the university, paid for the voyage himself—and went on to win the triple jump.

wrong anthem At the medal ceremony for the 1964 Tokyo Olympics marathon, won by Abebe Bikila of Ethiopia, the stadium band did not know the Ethiopian national anthem, so they played the Japanese one instead.

first gold India has 17 percent of the world's population, but the country did not win its first individual Olympic title until 2008 when Abhinav Bindra won the 10-meter air rifle shooting event.

bully-off As a reward for winning gold in the women's field hockey tournament at the 1980 Moscow Olympics, every member of the Zimbabwe team was presented with a live ox on their return home.

walk, don't run The three leading competitors in the women's 20-km walk at the 2000 Sydney Olympics were all disqualified for running in the final kilometer, leaving China's Wang Liping to claim an unlikely gold medal.

dirty laundry Competitors at the modern Olympics produce over 2,000,000 lb (907,000 kg) of dirty laundry. A family of four would take an estimated 264 years to get through that much laundry.

nine-hour bout The light-heavyweight Greco-Roman wrestling final at the 1912 Stockholm Olympics between Anders Ahlgren of Sweden and Ivar Böhling of Finland went on for nine hours without a decision being reached. So the judges called it a draw and awarded both men silver medals as neither had defeated his opponent to earn gold.

no gold Long-jumper Robert LeGendre, a 26-year-old graduate from Georgetown University, Washington, D.C., jumped farther than anyone else and set a new world record of 25 ft 5½ in (7.76 m) at the 1924 Olympics—but he didn't win a gold medal because he was competing in the pentathlon, where he could finish only third overall.

OLYMPIC HEROES

unbelievable feats

Ripley's
Believe It or Not!

OLYMPIC HOWLERS

calendar chaos After spending over 16 days at sea, the U.S. team arrived in Athens for the first modern Olympic Games in 1896 believing that they still had 12 days to prepare for the competition. In fact, the Games started the very next day—the Americans had forgotten that Greece still used the Julian calendar and was therefore 12 days in advance.

joined picnic Exhausted by the heat of the 1912 Olympic marathon in Stockholm, Sweden, Japan's Shizo Kanaguri stumbled into the yard of a family who were enjoying a picnic and stayed with them rather than rejoining the race.

lost medal After winning a rowing gold medal at the 1956 Olympics, 18-year-old Russian Vyacheslav Ivanov quickly lost it. He threw the medal into the air in celebration, but it landed in the lake. He dived in but was unable to find it.

hot stuff To prepare himself for the heat of Rome, where he won the 50-km walk at the 1960 Olympics, Britain's Don Thompson kept the heat on at all times in his bathroom for 18 months—and ran up a gas bill of over £9,000. He returned home from his triumph to find that the gas had been cut off.

lost in translation American athlete Loren Murchison was left at the start of the 1920 Olympic men's 100 meters final in Antwerp, Belgium, because he didn't understand French. When the starter said "prêt" ("get set"), Murchison thought that the crouching runners had been told to stand up and was doing so when the starting gun went off.

missing gloves Moments before he was due to fight at the 1992 Barcelona Olympics, Iranian boxer Ali Kazemi was disqualified because he had forgotten his gloves.

feeling crushed Having arrived in Canada in preparation for the 1976 Montreal Olympics, the Czech cycling team lost all of their wheels and spare tires after garbage collectors mistakenly took them away to be crushed.

shot in foot U.S. Lieutenant Sidney Hinds won gold in the free rifle team event at the 1924 Olympics in Paris, shooting a perfect 50—despite having been accidentally shot in the foot partway through the competition when the Belgian rifleman positioned next to him threw his loaded weapon to the ground during an argument with an official.

pot luck Sweden's Svante Rasmuson was set to win the modern pentathlon at the 1984 Olympics until, a few yards from the finish of the cross country, he stumbled over a potted plant, placed there by the Los Angeles organizers to brighten up the course. Italy's Daniele Masala passed him to snatch gold.

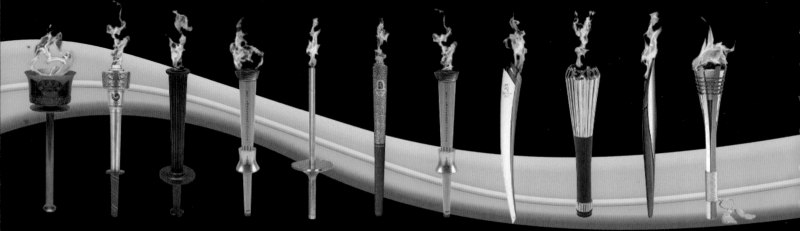

UNUSUAL OLYMPIC EVENTS

FAMOUS OLYMPIANS

- Lieutenant George S. Patton, one of the leading generals during World War II, finished fifth in the modern pentathlon at the 1912 Olympics.

- Johnny Weissmuller of the United States won three gold medals in freestyle swimming at the 1924 Olympics plus a bronze in the men's water polo, and two more swimming golds in 1928—feats that helped him earn a lucrative Hollywood career playing Tarzan.

- Buster Crabbe of the United States won a swimming gold medal at the 1932 Olympics and also went on to play Tarzan in the movies.

- Britain's Philip Noel-Baker won silver in the 1,500 meters at the 1920 Olympics—and in 1959 was awarded the Nobel Peace Prize.

- Crown Prince (later King) Constantine of Greece won a sailing gold medal at the 1960 Olympics.

- Hollywood actress Geena Davis took part in the trials for the U.S. archery team for the 2000 Olympics.

- Baby care expert Dr. Benjamin Spock was part of the Yale University eight that won rowing gold for the United States at the 1924 Olympics.

- Harold Sakata won a weightlifting silver for the United States in 1948 before going on to play the evil Oddjob in the James Bond movie *Goldfinger*.

- Princess Anne, daughter of Queen Elizabeth II, was a member of the British equestrian team at the 1976 Montreal Olympics.

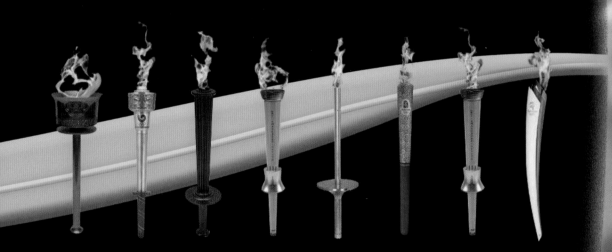

REMARKABLE TORCH RELAYS

Tokyo 1964 This torch relay featured the most torchbearers ever used—101,866—comprising a carrier, two reserve runners, and up to 20 accompanying people for every kilometer of its land journey.

Grenoble 1968 In the later stages of the relay, a diver swam across the French port of Marseilles holding the torch's flame out of the water.

Mexico City 1968 The relay retraced the steps of Christopher Columbus to the New World and featured one of his direct descendants, Cristóbal Colón de Carbajal, as the last runner on Spanish soil before the torch made its way across the Atlantic.

Montreal 1976 The Canadians organized the transmission of the flame by satellite between Athens and Ottawa by transforming it into a radio signal that was sent by satellite to Canada, where it triggered a laser beam to relight the flame on Canadian soil.

Lillehammer 1994 The flame was transferred between two parachute jumpers—in midair—and then made an impressive entry at the opening ceremony of the Games when it was carried by a ski jumper during his actual jump!

Atlanta 1996 and Sydney 2000
The Olympic torch (but not the flame) was carried into space by astronauts.

SHINE A LIGHT

One of the enduring symbols of the Games is the Olympic flame, which burns for the duration of the competition. A few months before each Games, at the Temple of Hera at Olympia, Greece—the site of the ancient games—a woman in ceremonial robes lights the torch, using just a mirror and the sun. The flame is then carried by relay to the host city, where it ignites the Olympic cauldron in the stadium and burns until the closing ceremony. During its journey, it must never go out. The route to each stadium is often long and tortuous.

In 2004, to celebrate the Games held in Athens, Greece, the torch went on a global tour, covering 48,470 mi (78,000 km) in the hands of some 11,300 torchbearers.

Over the years, it's been carried by dogsled, horseback, camel, and canoe, as well as by an army of runners.

When the flame has to travel in an airplane, special security lanterns are used, and every night of its journey the flame is kept burning in custom-made cauldrons, attended by three guards, one of whom must be awake at all times.

Eighteen authentic Olympic torches are displayed in the Ripley's Believe It or Not! Museum in London, England, among them the torch from the Sydney 2000 Olympiad that was carried, lit, underwater by divers near the Great Barrier Reef.

unbelievable feats

R **tennis marathon** At the 2010 Wimbledon Tennis Championships, John Isner of the United States beat France's Nicolas Mahut in a match that lasted more than 11 hours over three days. The match began at 6.18 p.m. on Tuesday, June 22 and finished at 4.49 p.m. on Thursday, June 24, Isner eventually winning 6-4, 3-6, 6-7, 7-6, 70-68 in a final set that lasted 8 hours 11 minutes.

R **mirror image** U.S. golfer Phil Mickelson is right-handed in everything but golf. He plays left-handed after mirroring his father's right-handed swing as a child.

R **every ground** In February 2010, Scott Poleykett from Kent, England, completed a 50,000-mi (80,000-km) journey to visit every soccer ground—professional and amateur—in England and Wales. In the course of his ten-year mission, he took photographs of 2,547 soccer fields.

R **commentator's nightmare** The finish of an August 2010 race at Monmouth Park, New Jersey, was fought out between horses named *Mywifeknowseverything* and *Thewifedoesn'tknow*. The two horses were unconnected, with separate trainers and owners.

TATTOO TRIBUTE

Colombian soccer fan Felipe Alvarez has had his upper body tattooed to resemble a jersey of his favorite team, Atletico Nacional. The tattoo is in honor of Andrés Escobar, the Colombian player who was shot dead as a result of scoring an own goal, which lost his side the match, while playing against the United States at the 1994 World Cup. Seen here with Atletico player Victor Aristizábal, Alvarez now has Escobar's number 2 permanently marked on his back.

R **one hand** At 6 ft 10 in (2.1 m) tall, Kevin Laue of Pleasanton, California, received a scholarship to play basketball for Manhattan College despite having only one hand.

R **flying shot** In 2010, Tyler Toney, a student from Texas A&M University, made a basketball shot he threw from a low-flying airplane!

R **atlantic crossing** A four-man crew led by Scotsman Leven Brown overcame 40-ft (12-m) waves, two capsizes, and an outbreak of food poisoning to row 3,500 mi (5,600 km) across the Atlantic from New York to the Isles of Scilly, which lie off the southwest coast of England, in 43 days in 2010. They were following the route of a Norwegian crew who had made the same crossing in 55 days back in 1896.

R **veteran coach** Soccer coach Ivor Powell finally hung up his boots in 2010—at age 93. A former Welsh international forward, he went on to train more than 9,000 players during his 53-year coaching career.

R **wrestling champs** In 2010, Blair Academy of Blairstown, New Jersey, won its 30th consecutive National Prep School Wrestling Championship.

R **monkey guards** Organizers at the 2010 Commonwealth Games in New Delhi, India, hired monkeys to work as guards at the athletes' village. They hoped that the team of 40 gray langur monkeys would chase off the packs of smaller rhesus monkeys that had been breaking into buildings and stealing from the competitors' quarters.

R **switch hitters** It took 134 years for the Arizona Diamondbacks' Felipe Lopez to become the first baseball player in history to switch-hit homers from both sides of the plate on Opening Day. It took just one inning, in the same 2009 game, for Tony Clark to become the second.

SAND SKIS

Germany's Henrik May prefers to ski on sand rather than snow—and in the Namibian Desert he reached a speed of 57.24 mph (92.12 km/h) while skiing down a 246-ft-high (75-m) dune. He has developed a special type of wax that enables the skis he uses to slide over sand.

flying fish One of the favorites to win the 2010 Missouri River 340—a grueling 340-mi (550-km) canoe and kayak race—Brad Pennington from Houston, Texas, was forced to quit just hours into the event after a 30-lb (13.6-kg) Asian silver carp leaped out of the water and hit him in the head. He described the blow as like being hit with a brick, and it left him with a pounding headache.

tug of war Fishing on the Victoria Nile River in Uganda, Tim Smith from Enniskillen, Northern Ireland, landed a 249-lb (113-kg) Nile perch, which at 6 ft (1.8 m) long, was taller than him. He battled for 45 minutes to reel in the monster—and then had to pry his catch from the jaws of a crocodile that launched itself at his tiny boat in a desperate bid to snatch the fish.

soccer saints An executive box at the Hamburg stadium of German soccer club St. Pauli is decorated like a Gothic chapel, complete with stained glass windows, candles, an altar to football, and depictions of the team's players as saints.

frozen toe The United States' Rulon Gardner, the 2000 Olympic Greco-Roman wrestling gold medalist, lost a toe to frostbite in 2002 and kept it in a jar in his refrigerator for years, apparently to remind him of his mortality.

free throws Perry Dissmore, a pastor from Hartford, Illinois, made 1,968 successful basketball free throws in an hour in September 2010—an average of one throw every 1.8 seconds.

matador fled Matador Christian Hernandez quit his job mid-bullfight in Mexico City in 2010—by running away from the charging bull, jumping over a wall, and fleeing the stadium to a chorus of boos.

loyal fan Nesan Sinnadurai, a United States-based fan of English soccer club Arsenal, has flown more than 6,000,000 mi (9,600,000 km) supporting the club since 1967. Every other weekend during the soccer season, the Sri Lankan I.T. consultant makes the 9,000-mi (14,500-km) round trip from Columbus, Georgia, to London to watch his favorite team.

blind abseiler Blind extreme sports enthusiast Dean Dunbar abseiled down the 658-ft-high (200-m) Eas a' Chual Aluinn waterfall in Scotland. He has also competed in power boating, mountain biking, sea kayaking, and hill running events, bungee jumped from a helicopter, and been hurled through the air as a human catapult.

super sprinter Irish sprinter Jason Smyth can run the 100 meters in 10.32 seconds—even though he is legally blind. He suffers from Stargardt's disease, a disorder that has reduced his vision to about ten percent of that of a fully sighted person, but can run so fast that he competed against able-bodied athletes at the 2010 European Championships.

too much yelling Manchester United goalkeeper Alex Stepney dislocated his jaw while shouting at his defenders during a 1975 soccer match against Birmingham City.

Sky Walker

Californian Dean Potter walked across a highline 100 ft (30 m) long and over 1,000 ft (305 m) above the ground in Yosemite National Park in 2009. He walked barefoot, and unattached. Dean has many years of experience on the highline—if he does slip off, he grabs the line with his arms or legs.

Ripley's Believe It or Not! Unbelievable feats

Stilt Stunt

In 1891, Sylvain Dornon from Landes, France, walked from Paris to Moscow, Russia, on stilts! He completed the 1,830-mi (2,945-km) journey in 58 days, averaging more than 30 mi (50 km) each day. Earlier in the 19th century, stilts were a fairly common means of getting around marshy terrain in certain parts of France, especially among shepherds, but, by 1891, Dornon was considered very strange indeed.

® **spinning yo-yos** At the 2010 London Toy Fair, Ben McPhee from Australia kept 16 yo-yos spinning simultaneously. He had yo-yos hanging off hooks, his fingers, and even his ears and teeth.

® **young climber** At just five years old, Sail Chapman of East Yorkshire, England, achieved his ambition of scaling all 214 peaks listed in Alfred Wainwright's famous Lake District guidebooks. He began walking the Cumbrian hills with his family at the age of two and completed the Wainwright peaks when he reached the top of his namesake fell, Sale, which stands at 2,536 ft (773 m).

NOSE-TO-NOSE

In March 2010, Robert Officer and John Milhiser from the Serious Lunch comedy group touched noses together for 10 hours 34 minutes, with no breaks or interruptions. Robert and John's record-breaking task included a trip on the New York subway and bathroom breaks together before appearing live on the Jimmy Fallon show.

UNDERWATER JUGGLER

With a single breath, Merlin Cadogan from Devon, England, was able to juggle three objects underwater for 1 minute 20 seconds.

® **tough granny** Pint-sized Sakinat Khanapiyeva, a 76-year-old grandmother from Dagestan, Russia, can tear through phone books, lift a 52-lb (23.5-kg) dumbbell while standing on a bed of nails, and break iron horseshoes. She first realized how strong she was at the age of ten when she moved a 660-lb (300-kg) box of grain—equal to the weight of four grown men.

wheelchair wheelie Nineteen-year-old Michael Miller of Ellington, Wisconsin, performed a 10-mi (16-km) wheelie in a wheelchair. Michael, who was born with spina bifida, completed 40 laps of a high-school track on two wheels in just under 4 hours. He performed his first wheelchair wheelie when he was just four years old.

text exchange Nick Andes and Doug Klinger, two friends from central Pennsylvania, exchanged a thumb-numbing 217,033 texts during March 2009. At the end of the month, Andes received an unexpected itemized bill for $26,000—for the 142,000 texts he had sent and the 75,000 he had received from Klinger.

happy hugger In Las Vegas, Nevada, on Valentine's weekend 2010, 51-year-old Jeff Ondash (a.k.a. Teddy McHuggin) of Canfield, Ohio, gave out 7,777 hugs in just 24 hours—the equivalent of more than five hugs a minute.

senior student Hazel Soares of San Leandro, California, received her college diploma in May 2010—at age 94! "It's taken me quite a long time because I've had a busy life," said the mother-of-six, who has more than 40 grandchildren and great-grandchildren.

tea potty Over a period of 25 years, Sue Blazye from Kent, England, has built up a collection of more than 6,000 teapots—and they take up so much room that she has converted her home (called Teapot Island) into a museum. Her favorite teapot is in the shape of Princess Diana's head, made when Diana got engaged to Prince Charles.

mayor moore Hilmar Moore has served as the mayor of Richmond, Texas, for more than 60 years. He was first appointed in 1949 and has been re-elected every two years since, although the last time he had an opponent was 1996.

bat breaker At the Riverwalk Stadium, Montgomery, Alabama—home of the Montgomery Biscuits Minor League baseball team—Steve Carrier broke 30 baseball bats over his leg in less than a minute. The 6-ft-4-in (1.9-m), 290-lb (131-kg) Carrier, from Dallas, Texas, also bends steel with his teeth.

Into the Skies

Aerial adventurer and qualified pilot Jonathan R. Trappe from North Carolina made history in May 2010 by traveling 76 mi (122 km) across the English Channel attached to a bunch of 55 helium balloons. Drifting from Ashford, England, toward France, Jonathan reached speeds of 35 mph (56 km/h) and heights of 7,000 ft (2,135 m). Three hours 22 minutes after taking off, and after a flight adjustment to avoid Belgium, he landed safely in a cabbage field near Dunkirk, France.

Ripley's Ask

Why did you first start balloon flying? I first became interested in balloon flight as a child—I wondered at a balloon, and how it floated upon the air. Then I thought "If I just get enough of these, couldn't I go into the sky?" As an adult, I left behind the idea that such a thing isn't possible and awakened a dream that had grown quiet.

What inspired you to cross the channel? The English Channel is a challenge that has called to aviators for generations. There is romance in flying over the famous White Cliffs of Dover and the Lighthouse at Dunkirk.

What was it like when you were in the sky? A quiet dream. I was 1,000 feet above the water and I could hear only the waves. When you're in the air, you move perfectly with the wind, not knowing where you'll land.

Was it a bumpy landing? The landing was smooth, but after the landing, as I worked to release the helium and take my balloons down, the winds kicked up!

What are your balloon ambitions? I would like to launch out of California, within sight of the ocean, and then fly inland, above the Sierra Nevada mountains, into the heart of America.

unbelievable feats
Ripley's Believe It or Not!®

everest landing British skydivers Leo Dickinson and Ralph Mitchell and Indian Air Force officer Ramesh Tripathi successfully landed their parachutes at an altitude of 16,800 ft (5,120 m) on Mount Everest in September 2009. After jumping out of a helicopter at 20,500 ft (6,250 m), they had just five seconds of free fall in which to open their chutes. The trio had to home in on Gorak Shep—a narrow, sand-covered lakebed and the only safe landing spot for miles around. "It was pretty hairy," said 62-year-old Dickinson. "If you missed that or overshot it, you were either going to die or end up with something important broken."

chopper leap Defying potentially dangerous turbulence, U.S. daredevil motorcyclist Travis Pastrana successfully backflipped a dirt bike over a helicopter that was hovering off the ground in front of Australia's Sydney Harbour Bridge, clearing the revolving chopper blades by about 13 ft (4 m).

paper round Ted Ingram has been delivering newspapers in Dorset, England, for nearly 70 years. He started his job in 1942 and estimates that he has since delivered more than half a million papers.

mass waltz More than 1,500 couples—from children to pensioners—danced a waltz in the main square of Tuzla, Bosnia, in 2010. Organizers estimated that as many as 25,000 people danced in the surrounding streets, but the square had to be sealed off so that the couples had enough room to move.

free haircuts Working round the clock, a team of ten stylists from Pump Salon completed 618 free haircuts in 24 hours in Cincinnati, Ohio, in September 2010.

old scout Reg Hayes, 95, of Oxford, England, retired in 2010 after 87 years as a Boy Scout. He joined the 2nd Oxford Wolf Cub pack in 1923 and moved up to the SS Mary and John 2nd Oxford Scouts in 1930, where he stayed for the next 80 years.

human wheelbarrow In Helsinki, Finland, Adrian Rodrigues Buenrostro from Mexico and Sergiy Vetrogonov from Ukraine completed a 131-ft (40-m) human wheelbarrow race in just 17 seconds.

car wash Students from Bloomington High School South, Indiana, cleaned 1,207 cars in ten hours in a marathon car-wash.

STILL LIFE
S.C. Naganandaswamy of Karnataka, India, can float in 20 ft (6 m) of water for 22 hours continuously without moving any limbs.

bulky wear Croatia's Kruno Budiselic managed to wear 245 T-shirts—ranging in size from medium to extra large—at the same time. The extra clothing added around 150 lb (68 kg) to his overall weight.

king gnome Andy and Connie Kautza of Wausau, Wisconsin, built a concrete garden gnome that stands 15 ft (4.5 m) tall and weighs more than 3,500 lb (1,590 kg).

HUMAN SPARKLER
Dr. Peter Terren of Bunbury, Western Australia, shot more than 200,000 volts of electricity down his body to create a spectacular version of Rodin's *The Thinker*. He turned himself into a human sparkler for 15 seconds by using a homemade Tesla coil, which transforms a feed of domestic electricity into a supercharged bolt of power. He was saved from electrocution by wrapping his torso, arms, and legs in builders' insulating foil—the electricity traveled through the foil and out to the earth from his foot. He also wore a tin-foil cap and a wire-mesh mask, and taped steel wool to the bottom of his left shoe to create the shower of sparks from his foot.

backward running Germany's Achim Aretz ran 10,000 m backward in a time of 41 minutes 26 seconds at the third Retrorunning World Championships in Kapfenberg, Austria, on August 8, 2010.

beach towel A beach towel covering a whopping 24,110 sq ft (2,240 sq m) of beach was unveiled near Las Palmas on the Canary Islands. A team of 25 people spent 15 days making the towel, and more than 50 people were needed to roll it out on the beach.

heavy suit U.S. Air Force Staff Sergeant Owen Duff ran a mile (1.6 km) in 9 minutes 22 seconds at Kirkuk Regional Air Base, Iraq, in 2010 while wearing an 80-lb (36-kg) bomb suit.

wheelchair crossing Setting off from his home in Lynn, Massachusetts, in June 2010, Matt Eddy crossed the United States by wheelchair in just over four months. Matt has been confined to a wheelchair since the age of ten and suffers from Duchenne Muscular Dystrophy, as a result of which he is strong enough only to move two fingers and requires a ventilator to breathe. Traveling on the quieter back roads to reach his destination of Long Beach, California, he averaged at least 25 mi (40 km) a day.

Milk Man

New Yorker Ashrita Furman once walked more than 80 mi (130 km) around a track in Queens, New York, with a full milk bottle on his head.

Anthony Martin has been an escape artist for more than 30 years, during which time he has performed a number of truly death-defying stunts.

ANTHONY'S GREAT ESCAPES

- In 1984, Anthony escaped after being bound in 20 lb (9 kg) of chains secured with six padlocks and nailed inside a coffin. The coffin was tied twice at both ends with heavy rope, weighted with rocks, and submerged in more than 6 ft (1.8 m) of water.

- After being chained hand and foot, tied with six sets of handcuffs, and locked behind six prison doors, he escaped from the Waushara County Jail in Wautoma, Wisconsin, in only 4 minutes 45 seconds.

- Wearing two sets of handcuffs and chained to the inside of a locked freight box, he was pushed out of an airplane at 13,500 ft (4,115 m) in 1988. He escaped at 6,500 ft (1,980 m) and parachuted safely to the ground.

- In 1990, he freed himself from a padlocked chain while locked in a metal cage submerged in icy water in 1 minute 45 seconds.

- Bound with handcuffs, he leaped from an airplane at 11,000 ft (3,350 m) above Idaho's deadly Snake River Canyon and, with just 30 seconds to pick the lock and open the parachute, he successfully escaped in free fall and landed on the north rim.

- Handcuffed in a chain of 12 handcuffs that included a 20-lb (9-kg) ball and chain, Anthony was locked in a cell at the Porter County Jail, Indiana, in 2009. He overcame the handcuffs and three locked jail doors to walk free in 8 minutes 13 seconds.

But if you think these are amazing...

TURN THE PAGE...

LEAP OF FAITH

Escape artist and evangelist Anthony Martin performed a daring skydive from an airplane flying at 13,500 ft (4,115 m) over Illinois—wearing handcuffs that were locked to a chain around his neck and linked to leather cuffs fastened above each elbow.

To add to the stunt's death-defying nature, the safety device attached to his parachute that automatically deploys the chute at 700 ft (215 m) was turned off. Without this backup, he had just 45 seconds, while spinning to Earth at 180 mph (290 km/h), to free himself from the handcuffs and chains and to reach back to pull the release handle and activate the canopy.

Falling in a sitting-back position, Anthony seemed to struggle with the lock for about 25 seconds before working himself free and safely deploying the chute.

The 45-year-old from Sheboygan, Wisconsin, has been picking locks since he was a child and made his first authenticated escape at age 12, when he managed to work his way out of a regulation police straitjacket. He jokes that he comes from the "School of Hard Locks."

Since then he has broken out of a locked box thrown from an airplane, escaped from being buried alive beneath 2,000 lb (907 kg) of sand, and freed himself from a heavily secured coffin submerged underwater. He has even requested permission to break out of Fort Knox—where most of the U.S. gold bullion reserves are stored—but the U.S. Government refused to allow the escape bid.

How did you first get into escapology? I became interested in escapes as a result of becoming disappointed in magicians' tricks. Although I can appreciate the talent required to do tricks, I didn't want to fool people—I wanted to do something real. With the proper tools and training, locks can be legitimately compromised. My goal is to thrill, not deceive.

What was your first escape? It was around the age of six, with the help of my ten-year-old cousin. He used to padlock a chain around my wrists from which I would try to escape.

Which has been your most dangerous escape? Aerial escapes, whether in a box or not, are always the most dangerous. Once you leave the airplane there is no going back.

Have you ever thought during an escape that you weren't going to come out alive? There have been times in my career when I did not have 100 percent certainty that I was going to make it unscathed. However, I never thought I would fail and pay the ultimate price. If I believed that, I simply wouldn't do it.

What went through your mind when you jumped from the airplane? When I am "in the zone" and in the middle of an escape, I am thinking of nothing but the required tasks that must take place to succeed. Everything else is blocked out of my mind, yet I always seem to have an internal clock that knows how much time I have.

How difficult was it trying to focus on your hands while you were spinning in midair? The difficulty of a skydiving spin is that centrifugal force wants to take my eyes off the work I need to do. Sometimes in these situations I can alter the position of my legs and stop the spin, but that requires me to divide my attention (something I don't like to do).

How do you prepare for your escapes? When preparing for an escape, I practice with the specific type or model of restraint I expect to be facing. This process can take several weeks to several months depending on the complexity of the stunt.

How satisfying is it to break free from a seemingly impossible situation? The Great Escape strikes a cathartic cord in all of us. How many of us haven't been in a sticky situation we wish we could get out of?

unbelievable feats
Ripley's Believe It or Not!®

shark incentive Spain's David Calvo solved two Rubik's Cube puzzles one-handed simultaneously in just 76 seconds while inside a tank with six sharks at the Terra Natura Park in Benidorm, Spain.

tightrope walk Chinese tightrope walker Adili Wuxor spent more than five hours a day for 60 days gingerly walking across a 1.3-in-thick (3.3-cm) steel wire strung across Beijing's Bird's Nest stadium at a height of more than 200 ft (60 m) above the ground. He walked about 12 mi (19 km) a day, so that he covered around 700 mi (1,130 km) in total.

gorilla run More than 1,000 people dressed in gorilla suits to take part in the 2009 Denver Gorilla Run, a 3½-mile (5.6-km) charity run/walk through the streets of the city to help mountain gorilla conservation.

poker session Professional poker player Phil Laak of Los Angeles, California, played poker for more than 115 hours from June 2 to June 7, 2010, at the Bellagio Hotel in Las Vegas, Nevada. He finished $6,766 up.

hang tough Strapped into special gravity boots and hanging upside down from a frame, Zdenek Bradac from the Czech Republic juggled three balls for 2 minutes 13 seconds, during which time he made 438 consecutive catches.

california wingwalk Traveling at speeds of 100 mph (160 km/h), often in the face of strong winds, Ashley Battles of Tulsa, Oklahoma, stood on the wing of a biplane for more than four hours in June 2010. Her wingwalk took place over San Francisco, California, giving her fabulous views of the Golden Gate Bridge and Alcatraz.

speedy mower Don Wales drove a lawn mower at a speed of more than 87 mph (140 km/h) at Pendine Sands in Wales, in May 2010. His grandfather, Sir Malcolm Campbell, broke the world land speed record, in a car, at the same venue in 1924.

stiletto sprinters Running along a 263-ft (80-m) course at Circular Quay in Sydney, New South Wales, Australia, a relay team comprising four women from Canberra— Brittney McGlone, Laura Juliff, Casey Hodges, and Jessica Penny—completed the four legs in 1 minute 4 seconds—while wearing 3-in-high (7.5-cm) stiletto heels.

bathtub voyage Rob Dowling of Dublin, Ireland, sailed 500 mi (800 km) down the Amazon River in a motorized bathtub in 2006. The 5-ft-7-in (1.72-m) fiberglass tub was supported by six 36-gal (136-l) steel drums and propelled by a 15-horsepower motor. He had intended to sail from Iquitos in Peru to the Atlantic—2,465 mi (3,967 km)— but his journey ended after just over 500 mi (800 km) when Brazilian authorities told him he didn't have a licence for the bathtub!

Ice Bath

Wearing only swimming trunks, Jin Songhao and Chen Kecai immersed themselves in ice up to their necks for 120 minutes and 118 minutes, respectively, high up on Tianmen Mountain in China's Hunan Province in January 2011. Jin was even able to write Chinese calligraphy during his ordeal.

lunge runner Jamasen Rodriguez of Modesto, California, is an expert in lunge running, where instead of running, the athlete lunges to his knees, alternating left and right with each step. In August 2010, he completed a lunge mile in just more than 25 minutes, taking 1,370 lunges.

human dominos Thousands of people in Ordos, Inner Mongolia, China, formed a human domino chain. Arranged in lines, the 10,267 participants slowly fell backward onto each other in sequence from a sitting position like a line of toppling dominos.

back handsprings At Valmeyer, Illinois, 13-year-old Chelsey Kipping did 32 consecutive back handsprings. She has been doing gymnastics since age four and practices for at least nine hours a week.

harley jump California stunt rider Seth Enslow jumped 183 ft 8 in (56 m) on a Harley-Davidson motorcycle near Australia's Sydney Harbour in March 2010. Three years earlier, the bike ace had performed a 200-ft (60-m) jump over a Convair 880 passenger jet airplane.

cat statues Winnie Ferring has a collection of more than 1,000 cat statues arranged on every available space inside and outside her home in Lansing, Iowa. She has been collecting them for more than 50 years, and each piece is numbered and documented.

africa trek French adventurers Alexandre and Sonia Poussin spent three years walking 8,700 mi (14,000 km) from Cape of Good Hope, South Africa, to Israel, living solely on the hospitality of people they met along the way.

trapeze veteran In his early seventies, Tony Steele still performed as a trapeze artist with the Gamma Phi Circus of Illinois State University, the oldest collegiate circus in the United States.

karate kid Varsha Vinod from Alappuzha, India, became a karate black belt in May 2009—the highest grade in the martial art—at the age of just five. She has been training since she was two and already has more than 15 katas, or karate disciplines, to her name.

manhole museum Stefano Bottoni has collected manhole covers from across the world—including from Holland, Finland, Cuba, the Czech Republic, Austria, and Romania—for exhibition at his International Manhole Museum in Farrara, Italy.

liberty walk French high-wire walker Didier Pasquette crossed a 150-ft-long (46-m) wire tied between two replicas of the Statue of Liberty on top of the 23-story Liberty Building in Buffalo, New York State, in September 2010. The feat took him about three minutes, and he stopped twice during his walk to wave to the crowds on the ground some 230 ft (70 m) below.

ball control Twenty-five-year-old schoolteacher Rohit Timilsina of Kathmandu, Nepal, managed to hold 21 standard tennis balls on the palm of his hand for more than 14 seconds in 2008. It took him three years of practice to achieve the feat.

Balancing Act

One man rode a bicycle 165 ft (50 m) along a tightrope suspended 26 ft (8 m) above a tiger enclosure while another hung below him on a ladder at China's Changzhou Yancheng Zoo in March 2010. The pair, who were part of a stunt that involved a three-year-old girl walking the rope behind them, narrowly avoided tragedy when one of the zoo's Siberian tigers leaped high off the ground and grabbed at the ladder, nearly causing the men to fall into the enclosure.

HOCKEY HORROR

Buffalo Sabres' goaltender Clint Malarchuk narrowly escaped death after a collision caused a player's skate to cut the carotid artery in his neck during a 1989 hockey match against the St. Louis Blues. If the skate had hit Malarchuk $1/8$ in (3 mm) higher, he would have been dead within two minutes. The injury was so horrific that 11 fans fainted and two had heart attacks, while three players vomited on the ice. Malarchuk needed 300 stitches to fix the wound, but was back playing in goal ten days later.

These heroic athletes and fans have the scars to show how sport can be dangerous. Incredibly, all have survived and, believe it or not, returned to the arena for more.

When baseball player Kelly Shoppach of the Cleveland Indians let the bat slip at a game against the Texas Rangers in Arlington, Texas, in 2006, this unfortunate fan failed to notice Shoppach's bat flying straight toward his face. In 2009, Shoppach claimed another victim when he struck a female fan in the face with a foul ball during a game against the Kansas City Royals.

FACEBALL BAT

MOST DANGEROUS SPORTS IN THE U.S.A.

(Injuries per year)

1. Basketball 512,213
2. Cycling 485,669
3. Football 418,260
4. Soccer 174,686
5. Baseball 155,898
6. Skateboarding 112,544
7. Trampoline 108,029
8. Softball 106,884
9. Swimming/diving 82,354
10. Horseback riding 73,576

DANGEROUS RING

Celebrating a goal for Swiss team Servette in 2004, recently married Portuguese soccer player Paulo Diogo jumped on the stadium fence and caught his wedding ring on the top. When he jumped off, he left the ring and half his finger behind. To add insult to injury, the referee showed him a yellow card for time wasting as the doctors searched for the missing finger! Although doctors were unable to reattach the digit, Diogo quickly resumed his career.

UNLUCKY BREAK

Brazilian-born Croatian soccer player Eduardo suffered a horrific broken leg when playing for his club team, Arsenal, in England's Premier League in 2008. A tackle by Birmingham City's Martin Taylor left Eduardo's anklebone sticking through his sock and kept him out of the game for almost a year.

BRUTE FORCE

Spanish matador Julio Aparicio was gored through the neck with such force by a bull in Madrid in 2010 that the end of the animal's horn can be seen coming out of the bullfighter's mouth. The horn went through Aparicio's tongue and penetrated the roof of his mouth. His life was saved after two operations and, incredibly, he returned to the ring two months later.

DIVING BELLE

Seventeen-year-old Columbus, Ohio, diver Chelsea Davis smashed the bridge of her nose on the diving board while competing at the 2005 World Swimming Championships in Montréal, Canada. She was lifted on to a stretcher, her face covered in blood, but she never lost consciousness and was soon back competing.

HOT HOOD

The Russian Extreme Games in Moscow were an opportunity for some of the most daring and crazy stuntmen in Russia to compete against each other in such dangerous events as riding BMX bikes with flaming tires, setting themselves on fire, and riding on the hood of a vehicle as it crashed through an inferno.

unbelievable feats

UNDERPANTS MAN

Gary Craig from Newcastle, England, also known as the Geordie Pantsman, took 25 minutes to clamber into an incredible 211 pairs of underpants in an unusual charity challenge in April 2010. Gary initially planned to wear 200 underpants, but an Australian rival had achieved this landmark only a few days before, so Gary was forced to set his sights higher and find bigger pairs of pants. This caused problems, as the smaller the underpants the greater the pressure, making it a painful physical challenge.

stamp collector
Postman Alan Roy from Dorset, England, spent 70 years painstakingly peeling off two million stamps from envelopes. He soaked each envelope in water and then carefully removed the stamp with tweezers. His collection is so big it fills up 40 packing crates that stack as high as a house.

emerald hunter
Jamie Hill of North Carolina has dug up nearly 18,000 carats of emeralds in his home state since 1998.

pi chart
Using only a single standard desktop computer costing less than $3,000, French software engineer Fabrice Bellard calculated pi to nearly 2.7 trillion decimal places. The complex calculation took him 131 days.

beer house
In Schleiden, Germany, Sven Goebel spent three months building a five-room apartment made entirely from 300,000 beer mats. It featured a table, chairs, and a fireplace—all made of beer mats. After spending up to eight hours a day, seven days a week, on construction, he then had to knock down the finished building to prove that it had been held together only with static, not adhesive.

plane pull
In Jilin, China, in 2010, martial-arts expert Dong Changsheng took less than a minute to pull a half-ton airplane for 16 ft (5 m)—by a rope hooked to his eyelids! He had previously pulled a car with his eyelids but this was his first attempt with a plane.

Poker Face

Bai Deng from Shandong, China, can hurl a regular playing card so hard and with such accuracy that he can slice a cucumber in two. It's not as impossible as it might seem, given that in 2002 U.S. magician Rick Smith Jr. threw a playing card a distance of 216 ft 4 in (66 m) at over 90 mph (145 km/h).

human fly Jem Stansfield climbed the side of a 30-ft (9-m) wall of a school in Brighton, England, in 2010 using nothing more than suction from two vacuum cleaners. The 168-lb (76-kg) aeronautics graduate adapted the household appliances' motors into giant suckerpads, which were strong enough to support him and enabled him to cling to the wall.

flying lanterns More than 10,000 twinkling white paper lanterns were released simultaneously into the night sky from a beach in Jakarta, Indonesia, in December 2009. The flying lantern is a Chinese tradition. It is basically a paper bag containing a block of paraffin with a wick suspended by wire across the opening. When the wick is lit, the air inside is warmed like a hot-air balloon and the lantern lifts off into the sky.

rubber bands Eleven-year-old Allison Coach of Chesterfield Township, Michigan, created a chain of 22,140 rubber bands that stretched nearly 7,000 ft (2,130 m)—or 1.3 mi (2 km)—long.

champion plowgirl Thirteen-year-old schoolgirl Elly Deacon beat experienced farmers for first place in a plowing competition in Hertfordshire, England. Elly, who had driven a tractor for the first time only four days before the event, impressed judges with her straight and smooth plow marks on a 53,000-sq-ft (4,900-sq-m) patch of land, while at the wheel of the six-ton tractor.

turbo terry Terry Burrows from Essex, England, cleaned three windows, each measuring 45 sq in (290 sq cm), and wiped the sills in just 9.14 seconds during a 2009 window-cleaning competition in Blackpool, Lancashire. "Turbo Terry" actually finished the task in 8.14 seconds, but was handed a one-second time penalty for leaving two water marks on the glass.

rain dance More than 230 dancers took to the wet streets of Bath in Somerset, England, with umbrellas in May 2010 to perform a five-minute version of Gene Kelly's classic "Singin' in the Rain."

sand burial As part of the 2010 Clogherhead Prawn Festival in County Louth, Ireland, 524 people simultaneously buried themselves up to their necks on a sandy beach.

Page numbers in *italic* refer to the illustrations

ACKNOWLEDGMENTS

COVER (t/l) www.tesladownunder.com, (b/l) anthonyescapes.com, (r) Jeffrey Cunningham; 4 Jeffrey Cunningham; 6–7 Akash Awasthi; 8 © Akintunde Akinleye/Reuters/Corbis; 9 (t) AP Photo/Luis Benavides, (c/l, b/l, b/r) Swell.com; 10 (l) Iain Ferguson, The Write Image, (r) © Wifredo Garcia Alvaro/epa/Corbis; 11 Christian Pondella/Caters News; 12–13 © -M-I-S-H-A-/ iStockphoto.com; 16 (t) AFP/Getty Images, (b) Henrik May/ski-namibia.com; 17 Jeffrey Cunningham; 18 (b) Edmond Hawkins, (t) Getty Images; 19 Nick Obank/Barcroft Media Ltd; 20 (t) Nagananda Swamy, (b) www.tesladownunder.com; 21 (t/r) anthonyescapes.com, (b) Dan Callister/Rex Features; 22–23 anthonyescapes.com; 24 Qiu xiaofeng/AP/Press Association Images; 25 Quirky China News/Rex Features; 26 (t) Harry Scull Jr./AP/Press Association Images, (b) Ron Jenkins/ Fort Worth Star-Telegram/Polaris; 27 (sp) Eric Lafargue /www.LPS.ch, (b) Target Press/Barcroft Media Ltd, (t) Stephen Pond/EMPICS Sport; 28 (t/l, t/r) Stephen Pond/EMPICS Sport; 29 RYAN REMIORZ/AP/Press Association Images; 30–31 EPA/Photoshot; 32 The Shields Gazette; 33 ChinaFotoPress/Photocome/Press Association Images; BACK COVER Edmond Hawkins

Key: t = top, b = bottom, c = center, l = left, r = right, sp = single page, dp = double page

All other photos are from Ripley Entertainment Inc.
Every attempt has been made to acknowledge correctly and contact copyright holders and we apologize in advance for any unintentional errors or omissions, which will be corrected in future editions.